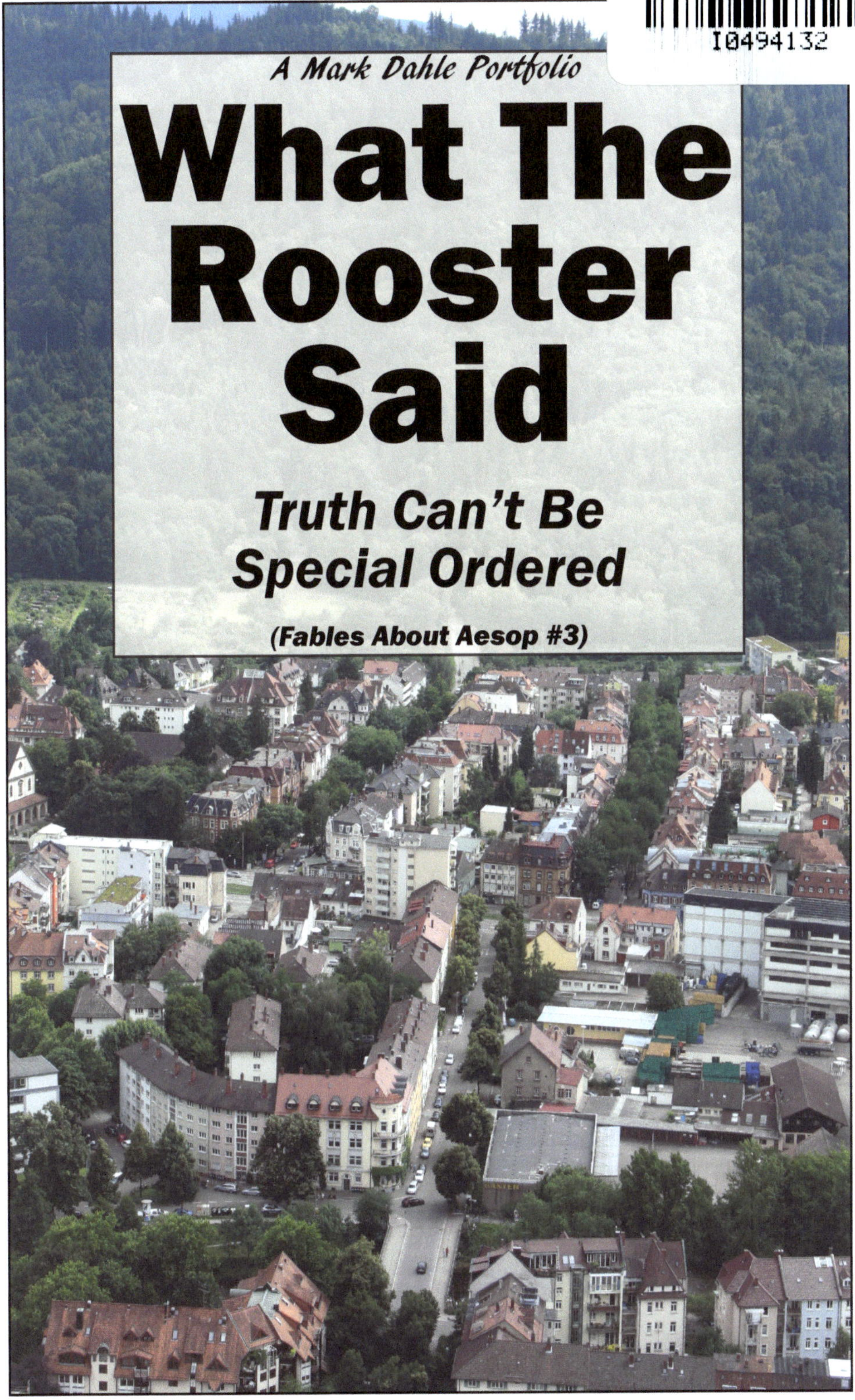

A Mark Dahle Portfolio

What The Rooster Said

Truth Can't Be Special Ordered

(Fables About Aesop #3)

*Mark Dahle has written many great fables about Aesop.
This is #3.*

~ ~ ~

*Mark Dahle Portfolios can be read in a few minutes and enjoyed
for a lifetime.*

*Unlike many picture books, the text is not related to the beautiful
painting at the right and the photographs that follow. This might
seem a little weird at first. One thing that helps is to order more
portfolios until you get used to it. In the meantime, feel free to
draw your own pictures of Aesop if you like.*

*This portfolio includes a photo of a brilliant 36 x 24 inch
painting (at the right), twenty-five beautiful pictures of Freiburg,
Germany, and a story about Aesop's early years.*

*Photographs in this book are available in very limited editions.
See http://www.MarkDahle.com for more information and for
previews of upcoming portfolios.*

*We do our best to create portfolios free of editing mistakes. But it's hard to
catch everything. We reward people who report errors in any Mark Dahle
portfolio. For details see MarkDahle.com/Typos.html or send an email to
MarkDahle@aol.com with the subject line "Typos." Thanks!*

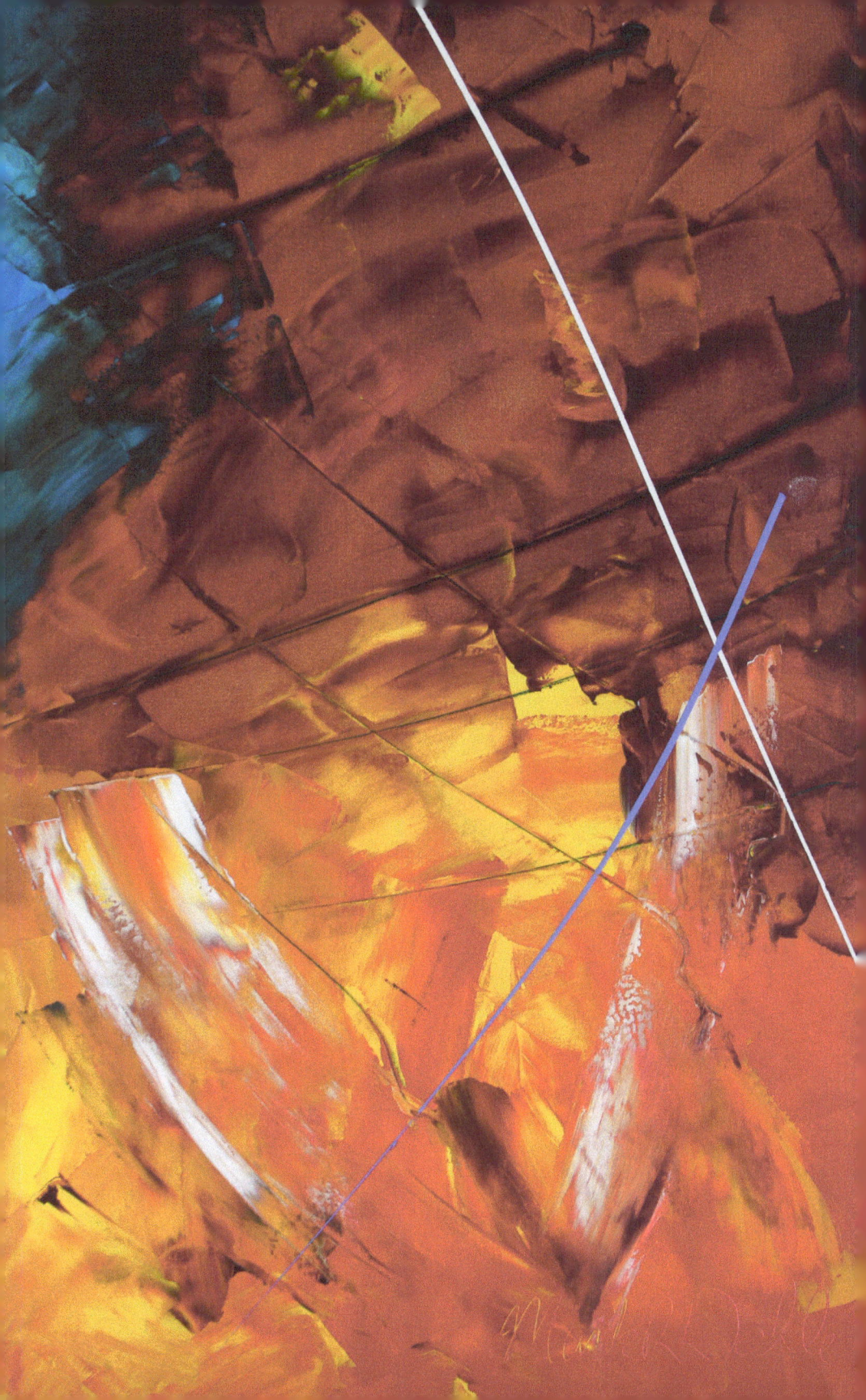

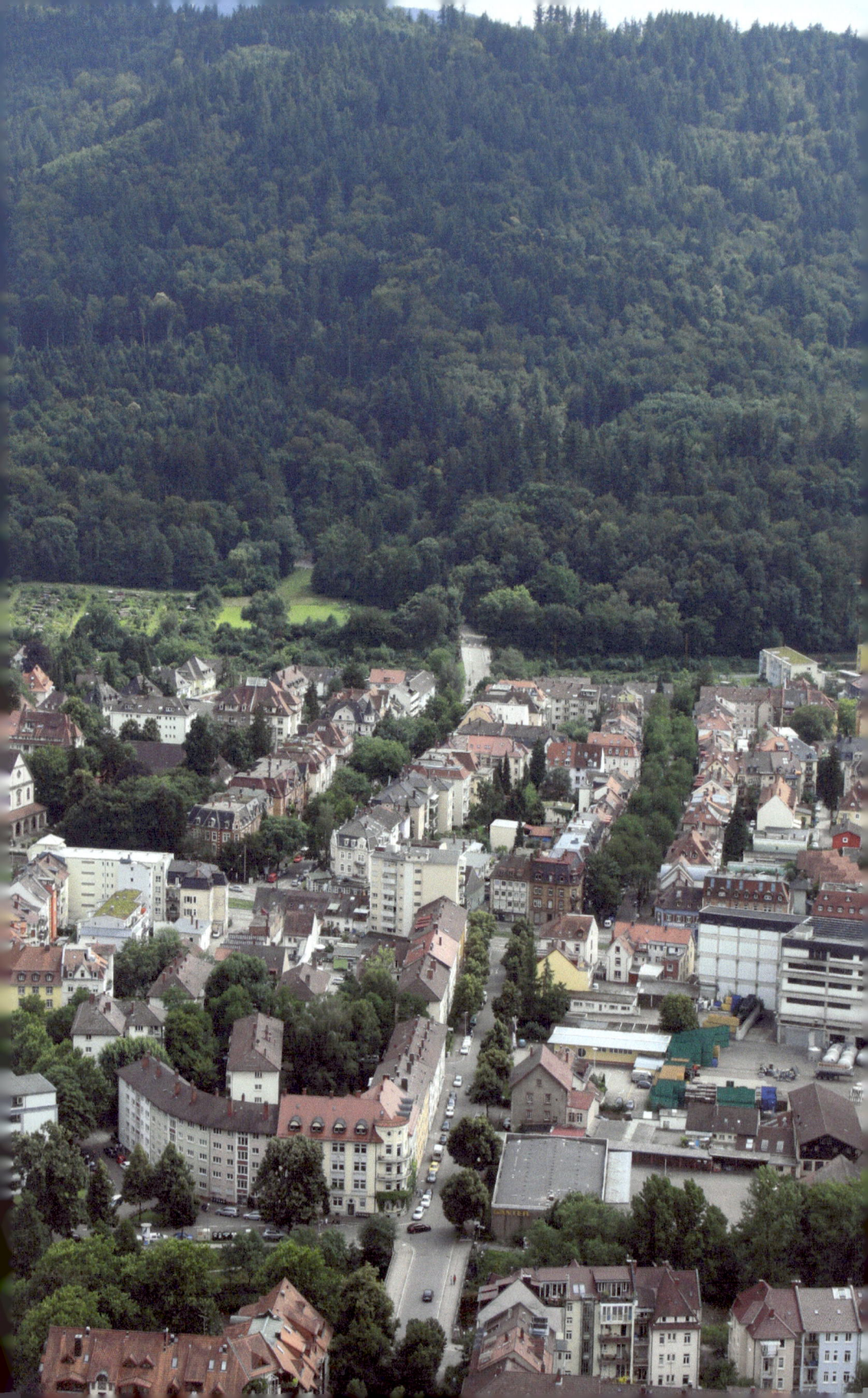

One day on his way home from school, Aesop found his path blocked by Javan and Damian.

"Where's Tad?" Aesop asked.

"He left," Javan said. "He said he had something to do. He also said he wanted us to listen to you. But he's gone. So get ready to get beat up."

Aesop had been trying to think of another story that might help him escape the bullies. He'd had a whole day to think about it. But he had nothing. Now he said the first idea that popped into his head.

"Do you know why the jackal ate his lunch?"

Aesop had seen a jackal on a long walk he took the day before, so maybe that's why the question came to him. But as soon as he said it, Aesop felt like kicking himself. What a stupid thing to say. He didn't even have an answer to the question. But it didn't matter.

"No," said Javan. "And I don't care."

Javan hit Aesop hard, in the stomach. Aesop fell to the ground. Damian kicked him, then he and Javan left, laughing.

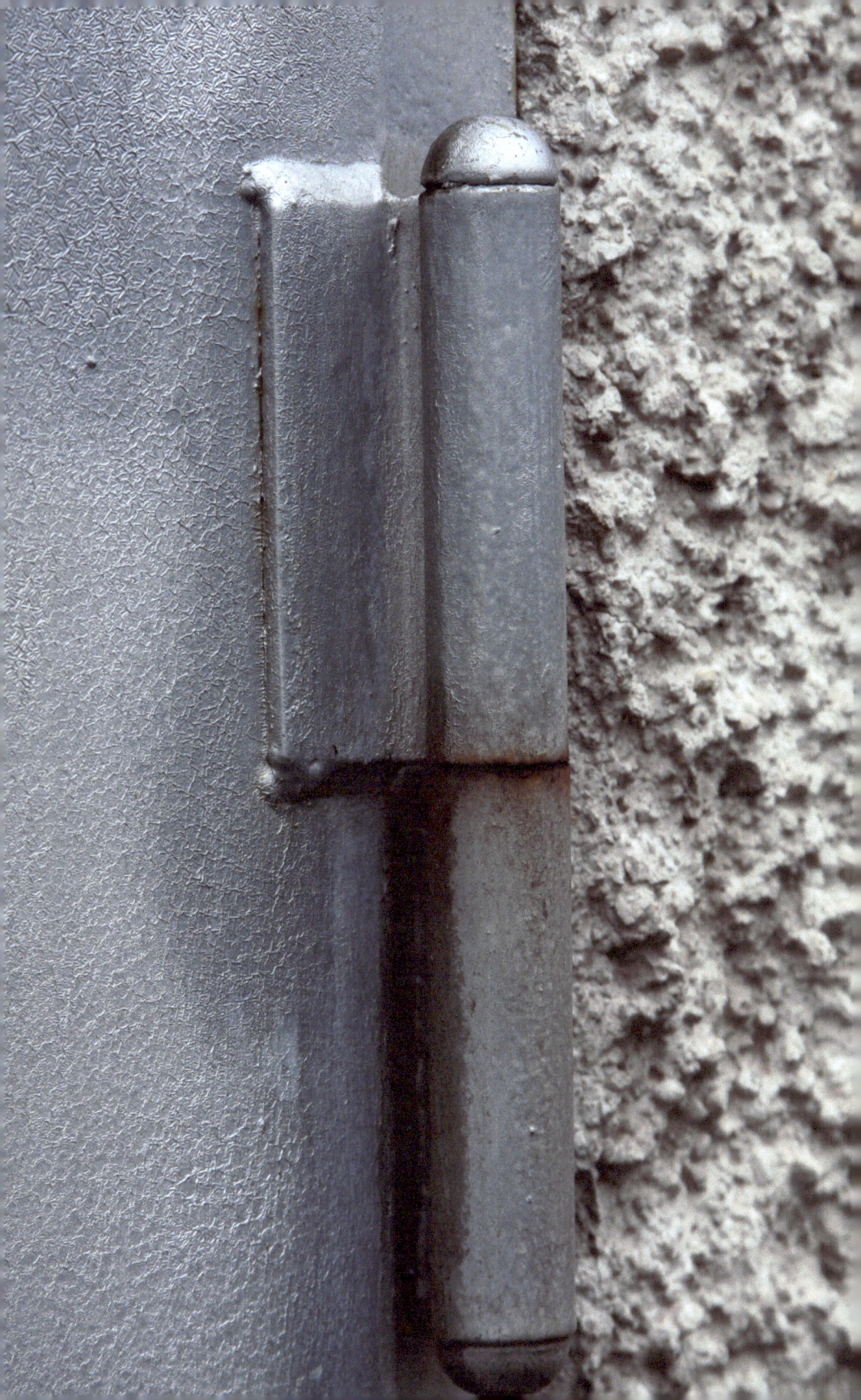

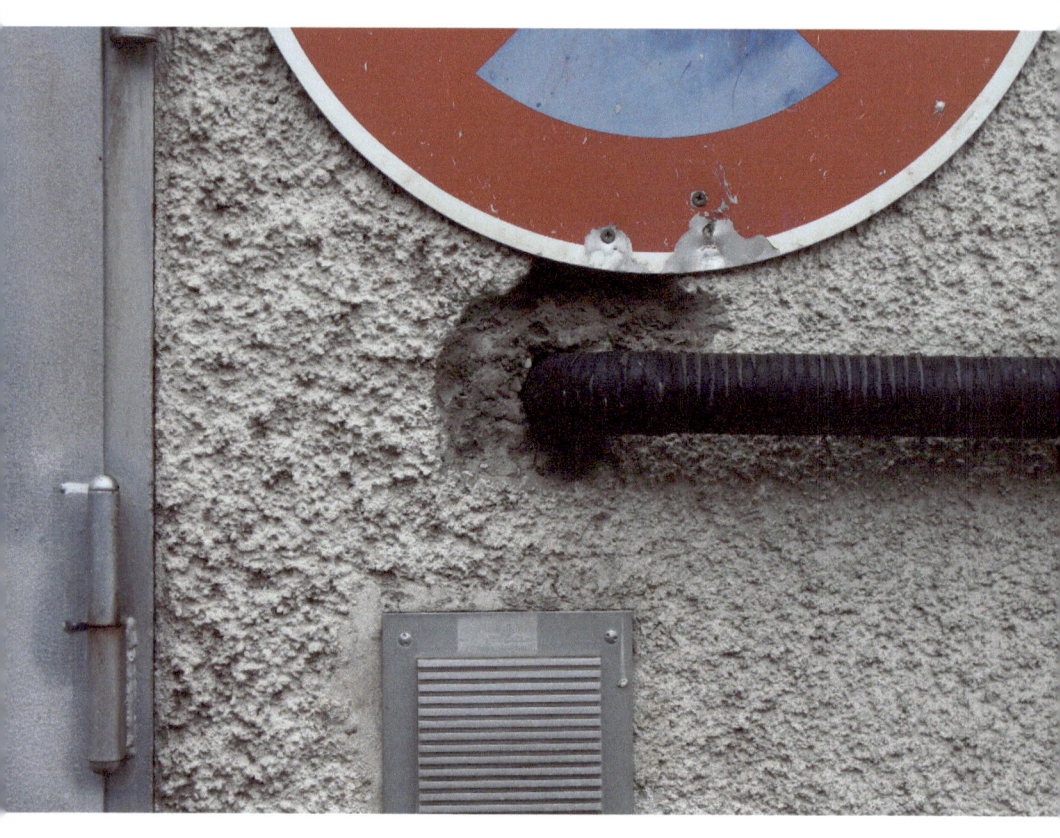

Nothing looked different about their encounter with Aesop compared with other days. But Javan was changed. He couldn't get the question out of his mind. He thought Aesop might be calling him a jackal. That made him mad, and he spent some time planning how he would ambush Aesop the next day. But every now and then the question would come back: Why *did* the jackal eat his lunch? It was a riddle he couldn't solve on his own. He couldn't solve it without Aesop.

Aesop, however, was unaware of this. He was miserable. He'd had a whole day to come up with a story to keep himself out of trouble and he'd been unable to do it.

He had, in fact, thought of plenty of stories. But none of them seemed enough to keep bullies away. Then, when he *had* blurted something out, he had still gotten beat up.

His stomach hurt from Javan's punch. He shin hurt from Damian's kick. *He* hurt from the pain of having no close friends. He hurt from the endlessness of the bullying. He hurt that Octavia wouldn't allow him to stay home.

"You can apprentice next year," she had said. "Until then, school it is."

Aesop wasn't sure he could take it for another year.

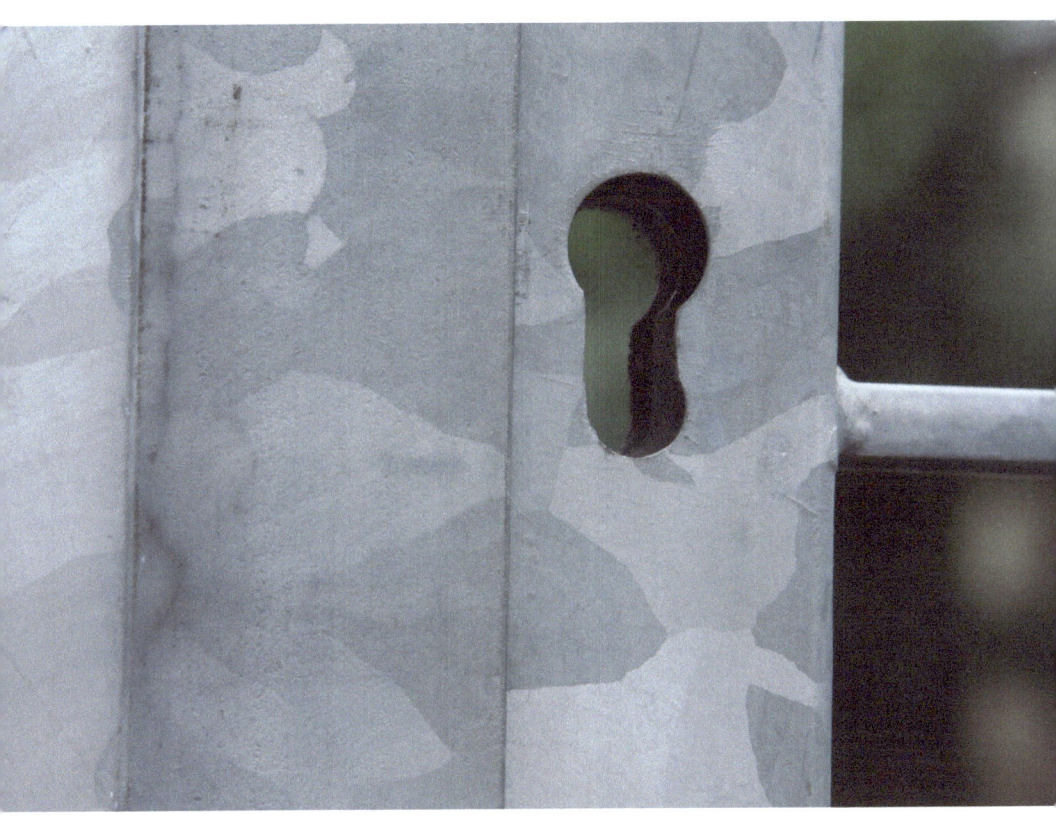

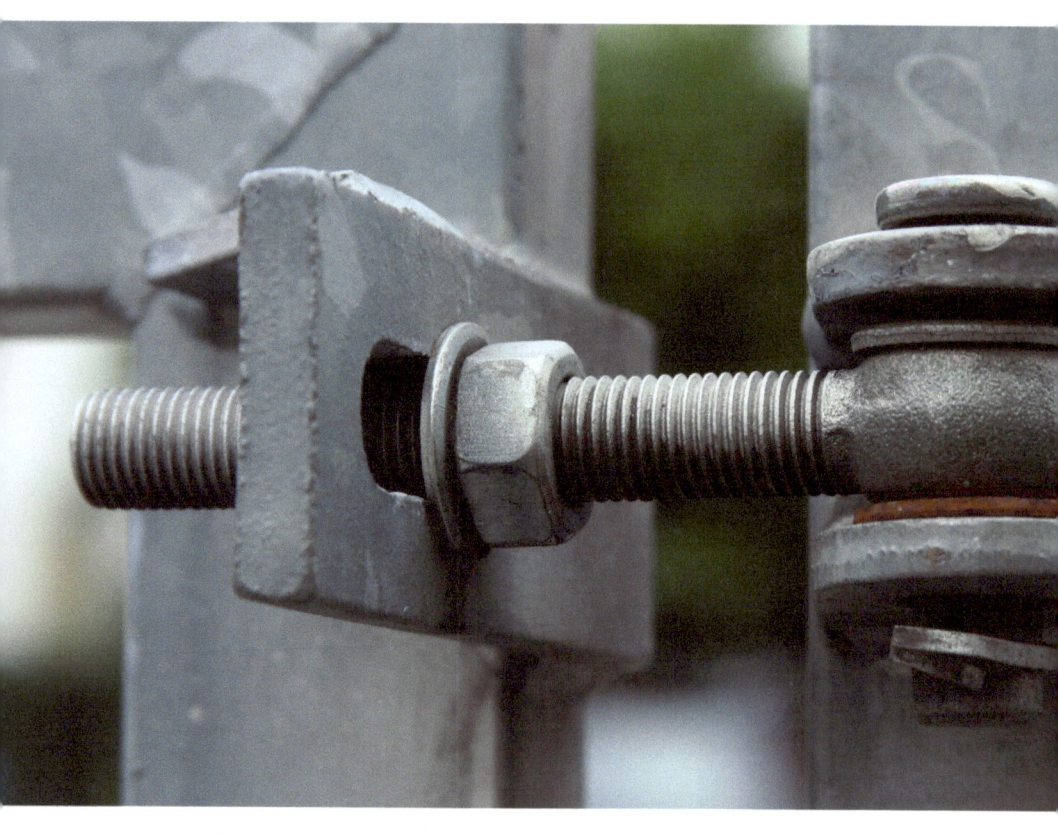

The next day Tad came up to Aesop at school. Aesop eyed him warily.

"Thanks for telling me about the frogs," Tad said. "I really like the swamp. I hadn't noticed how beautiful it was." Then he wandered off.

After school, Tad greeted Javan and Damian, then excused himself. He said he couldn't stay.

"At least wait until Aesop comes by," said Javan.

"I have to go," Tad said. "But say hi to Aesop for me."

"You want us to punch him for you?"

"What? No!" Tad laughed. "He's not that bad, Javan. You should listen to him."

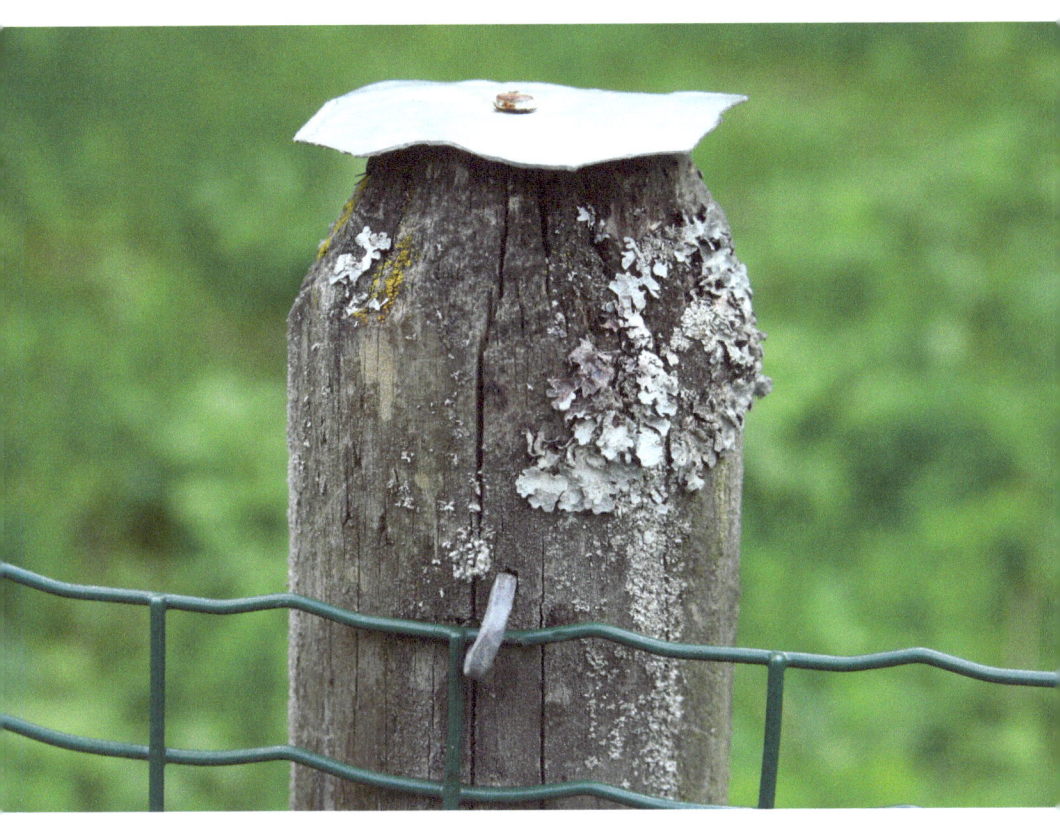

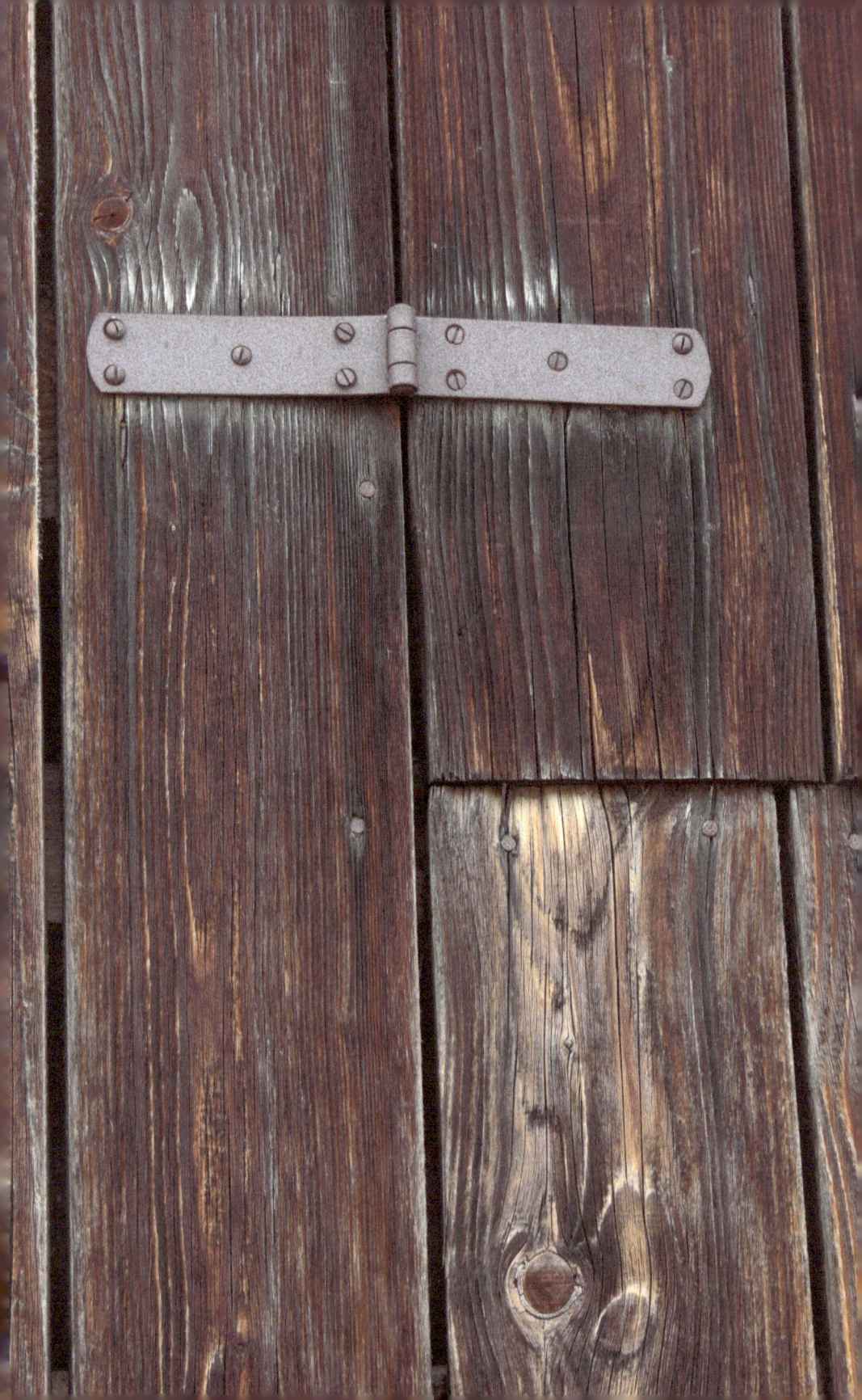

When Aesop came by, Javan was still steaming. "You better not break up our gang, Aesop," he said.

"Right," said Aesop. "How could I do that?"

Javan hit him in response, then Damian grabbed him and Javan hit him a couple more times.

When Damian released him, but before Aesop could limp home, Javan blocked his path. "Why did the jackal eat his lunch?" he demanded.

Aesop was hurting so much it didn't even register the turning point that had just happened. But he was in no mood to reply. It didn't matter, anyway. He had already been beat up. So why say anything? Aesop wasn't going to answer, even if it meant getting hit again.

Aesop pushed past Javan, perhaps his first defiant physical move with Javan ever. After a few steps he turned back. "I'll tell you tomorrow," he said. "At lunch."

Then he limped home.

Part of the problem for Aesop was that any answer to the question that he could think of wasn't that great – at least not great enough to save him from a daily beating. But as he limped home, it gradually dawned on him what a change had taken place: Javan was curious. Could Aesop come up with a better answer to the riddle? One that might keep him from being hit?

Aesop wrestled with the question all night, but he still could not solve it.

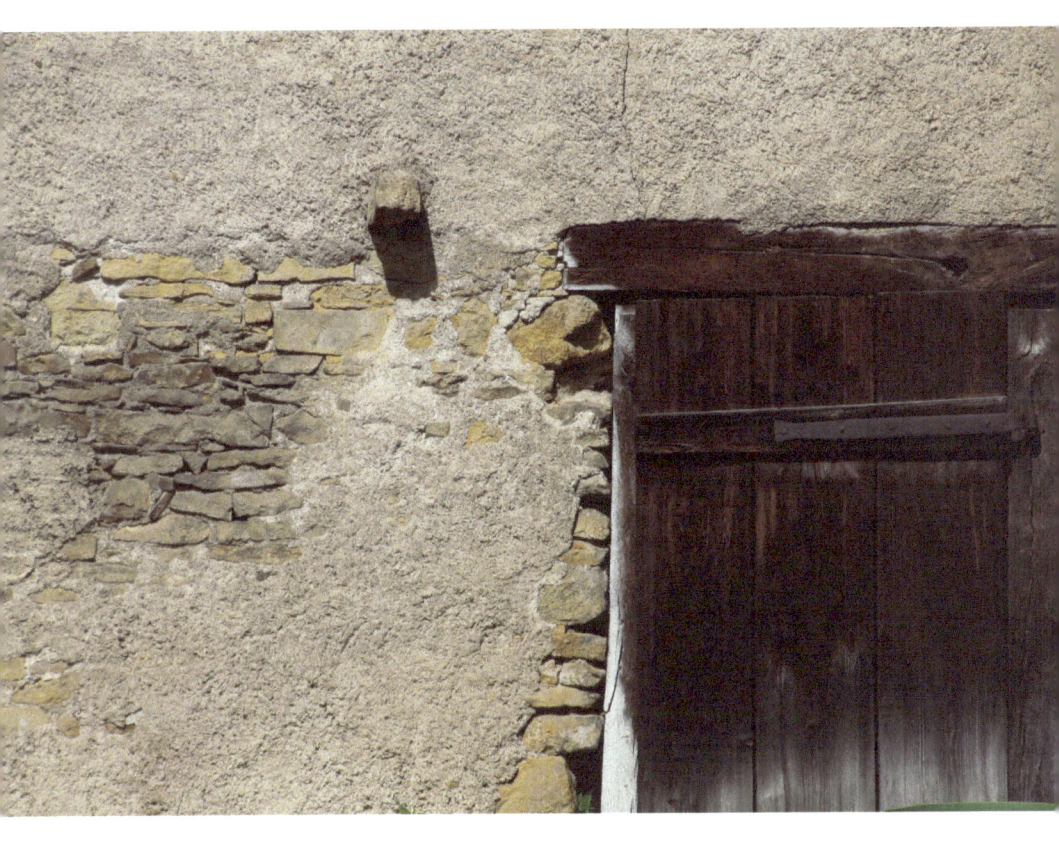

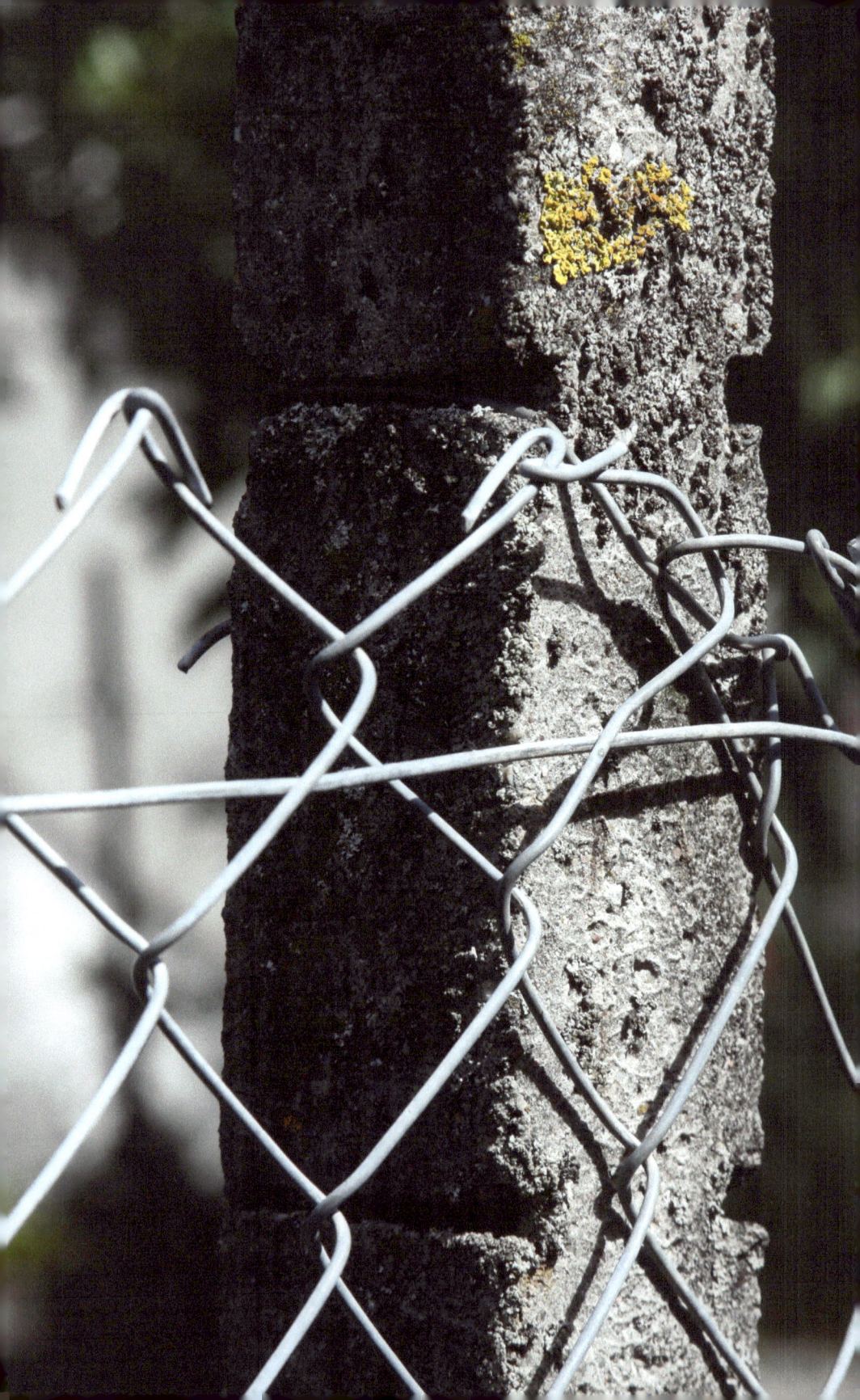

The next day Aesop barely noticed that Tad was missing. He was still desperately trying to answer his own riddle. He sweated through his morning classes and gave such poor answers his teachers thought he might be unfit for the group he was in.

When lunchtime came, Javan and Damian pushed Aesop into the center of the crowd of kids. This got everyone's attention. The bullies seemed to be working *with* Aesop, or at least advancing him. What could *that* mean?

Everyone stared at Aesop. Aesop himself stared at the ground. He still had nothing to say.

Prodded by Javan, Aesop blurted out what he had. "I have a riddle," he said. "Why did the jackal eat his lunch?"

His schoolmates looked at each other. This was unexpected.

Aesop glanced up. All eyes were on him.

"You probably don't know the answer," Aesop said. He was stalling. *He* still didn't know the answer, either. So he just said the first words that came into his head.

"It was because of what the rooster said."

Then he sat down. At least he attempted to. It was something between fainting and actually sitting on a chair. But his audience wouldn't allow it.

"What did the rooster say?" asked several voices.

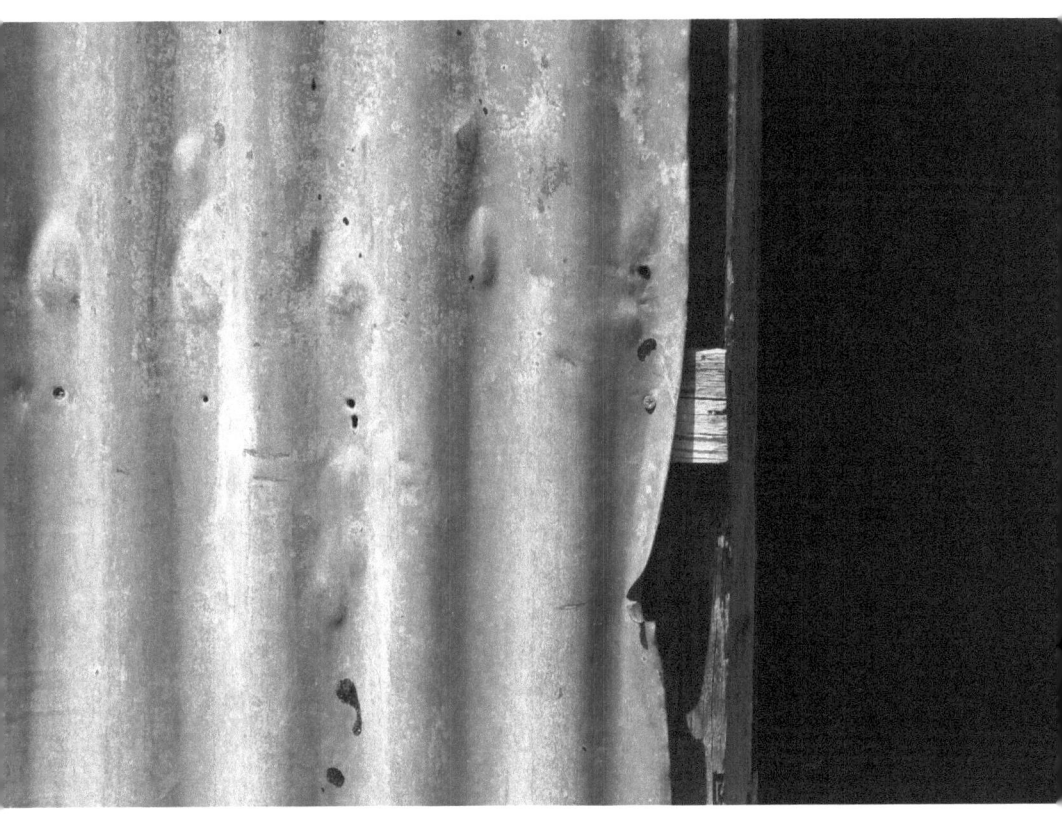

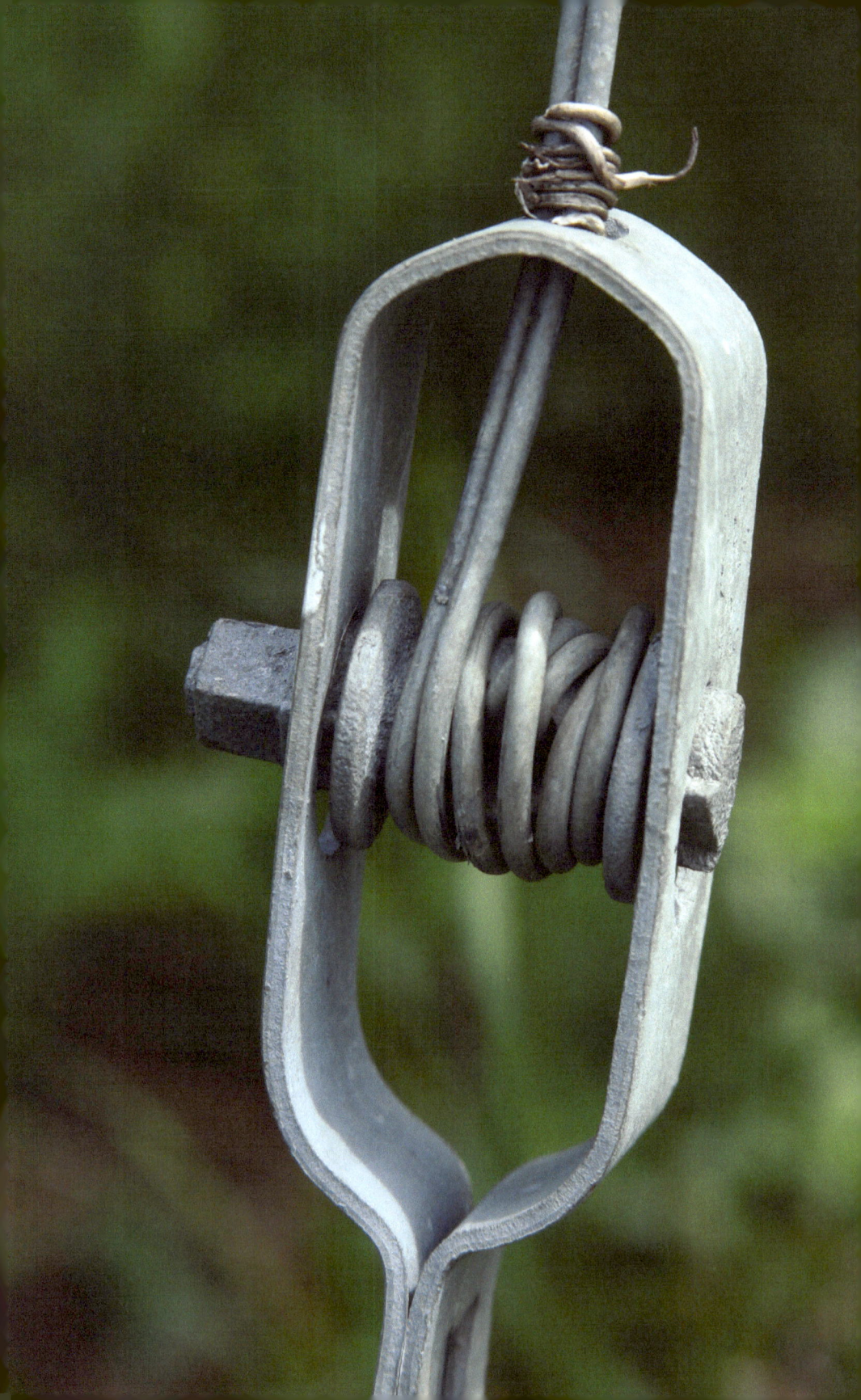

"I'll tell you at lunch tomorrow," said Aesop.

He was miserable, but he tried not to show it. He'd had another day to come up with an answer, and he *still* hadn't figured out his own riddle. Now he'd made it worse. He'd gotten everyone in school interested in a riddle he couldn't answer.

That day on his way home, Aesop didn't even try to hide from Javan and Damian. He walked right up to them. But to his surprise, they let him pass. "You better have a good answer tomorrow," Javan said. "Otherwise we're beating you up twice. Once for today and once for tomorrow. And maybe once for yesterday."

Aesop walked home in a daze. He was in a terrible spot. He had no answer for the riddle he had posed. But even so, it had saved him from getting hit, at least today.

At lunchtime the next day, Javan again pushed Aesop into the center of the students.

Aesop still had no answer that would satisfy. But by now the whole school was involved.

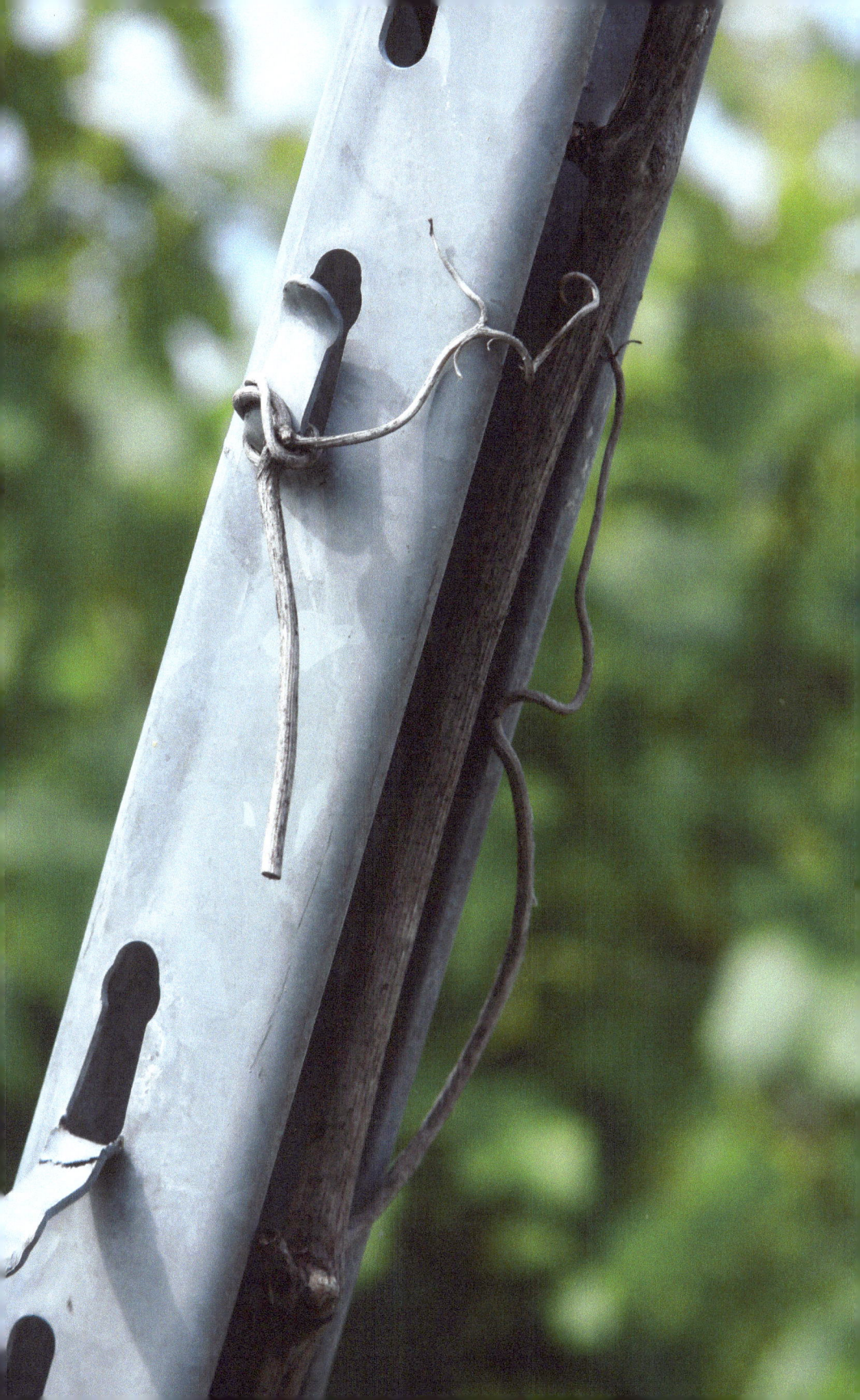

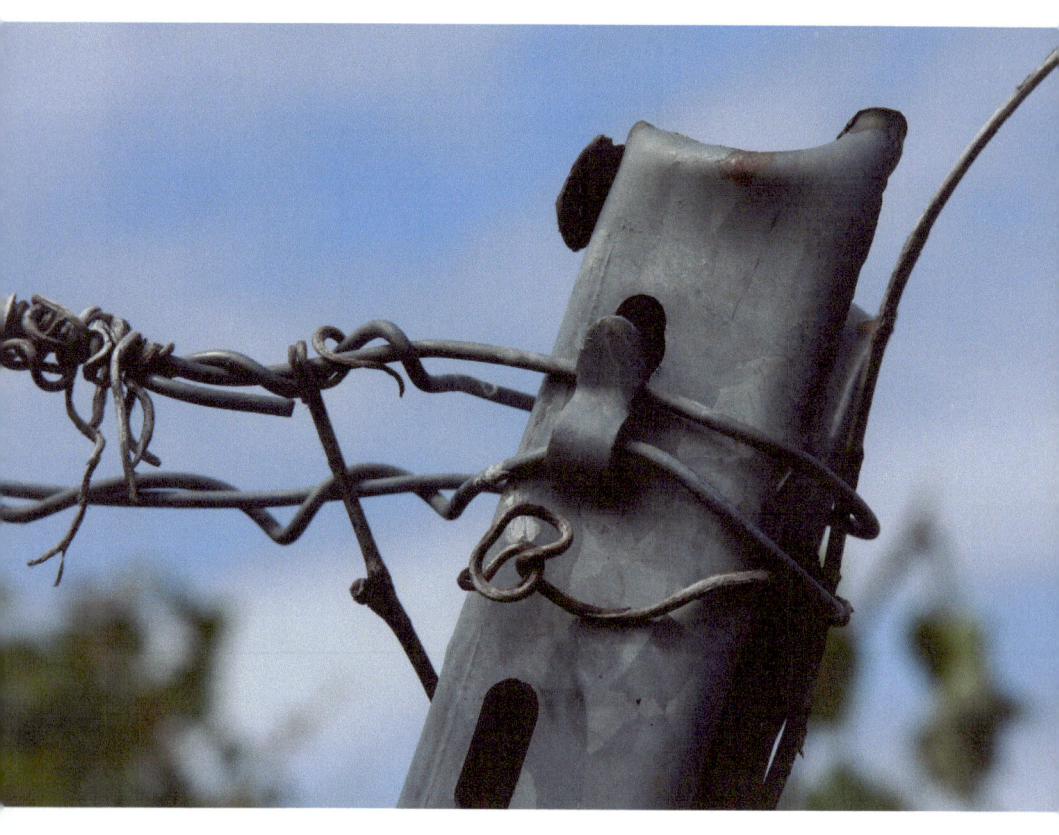

Staring at the ground, Aesop said, "I have a riddle. Why did the jackal eat his lunch?"

The response stunned him. All his classmates said, in unison, "Because of what the rooster said."

Aesop glanced up with hope until he remembered he still didn't know what the rooster said. He was going to be beat up while the whole school watched if he didn't work this out soon.

"You probably don't know what the rooster said," Aesop stammered. Again he didn't know what to say.

"The rooster said. . ."

Aesop paused, not for effect, but because he genuinely had no idea. Luckily for him, it had the effect of pulling his classmates in. Again he said the first thing that came into his head. "Truth can't be special ordered."

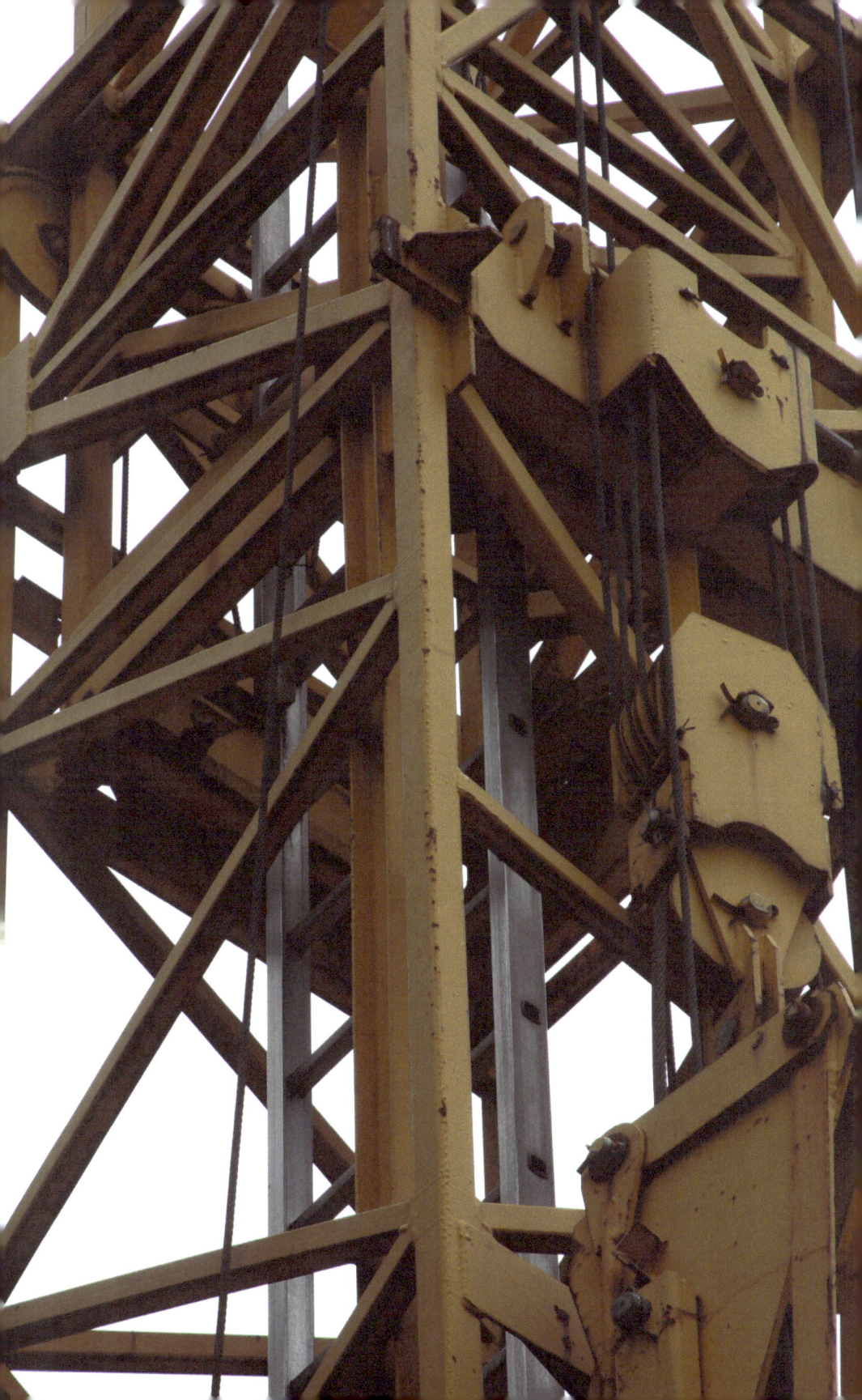

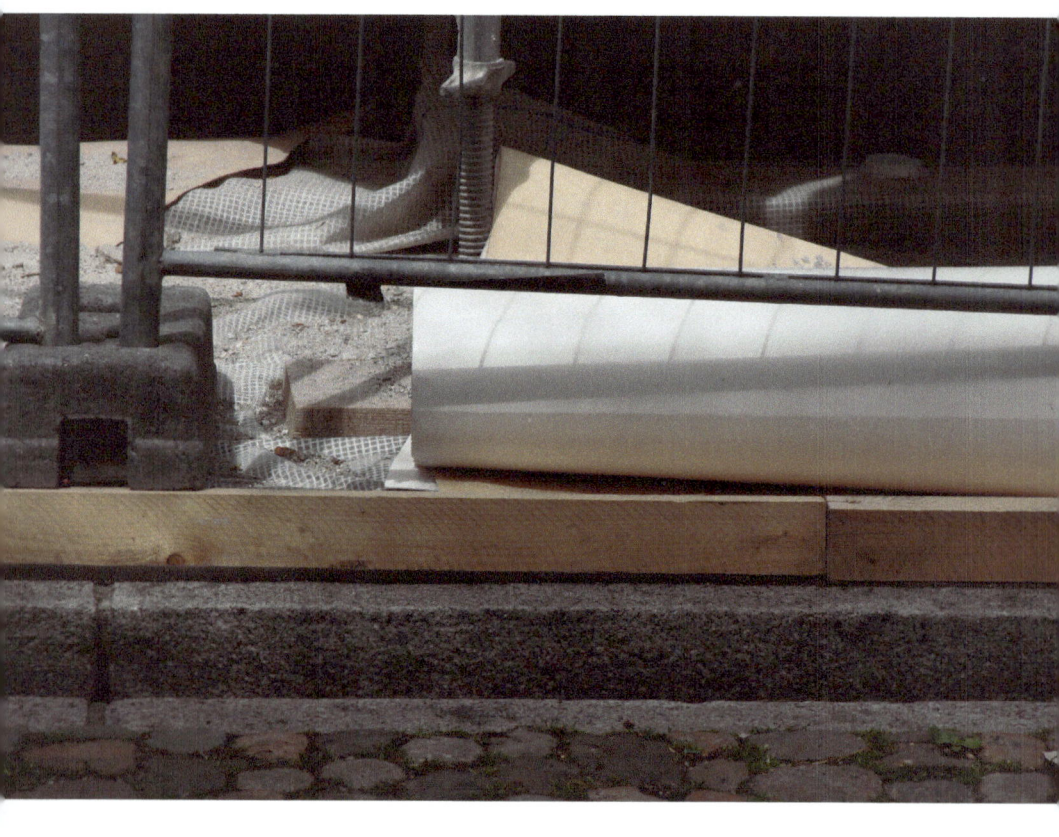

Aesop saw Javan tighten his fingers into a fist. But by now everyone else was playing along, thinking it a game and not realizing (or maybe not caring) how high the stakes were for Aesop.

"What does *that* mean?" called out a couple classmates.

"I'll tell you at lunch tomorrow," Aesop said.

On the way home, Aesop felt like throwing up. He was going to be beat up twice today by the bullies, and probably by everyone at school tomorrow. But he was no longer cowering. He walked straight towards Javan and Damian. To his surprise, they let him pass.

"Aesop," Javan said, "this better be worth it. If you mess up tomorrow, we're probably going to kill you."

Aesop looked Javan in the eyes, something he would never have done before. "Let me through," he said. "I'm not telling you what the riddle means until tomorrow." Javan stepped aside, and Aesop continued home.

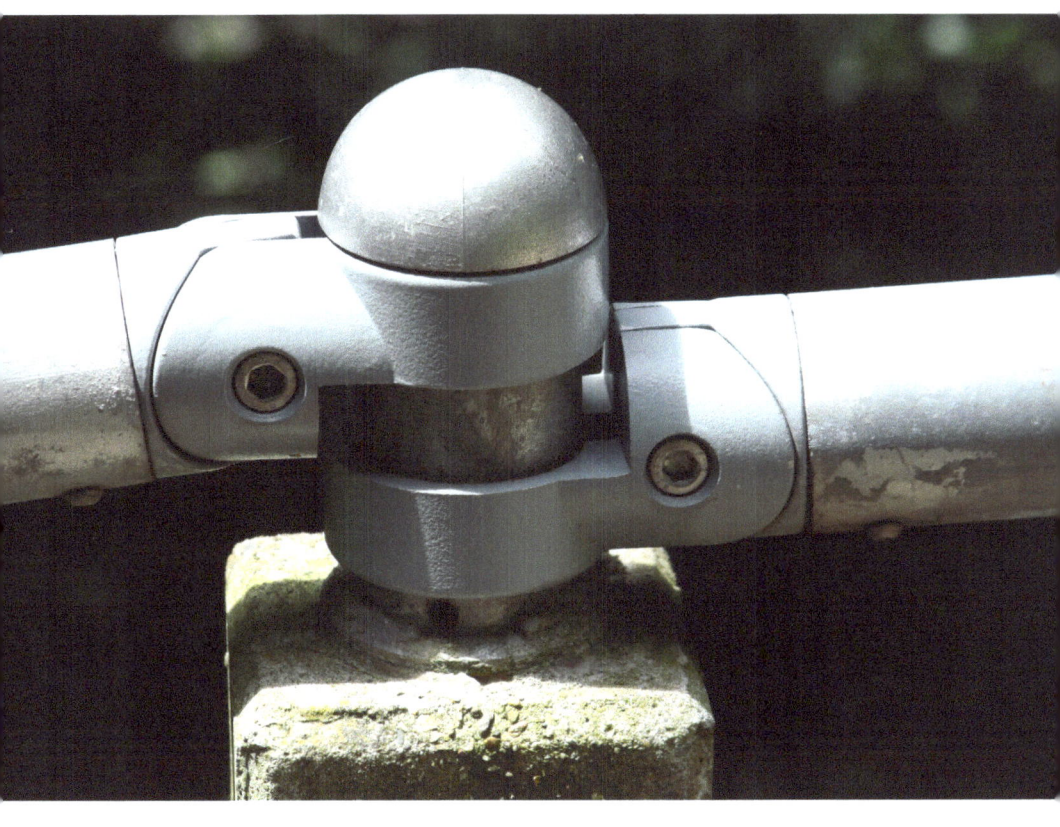

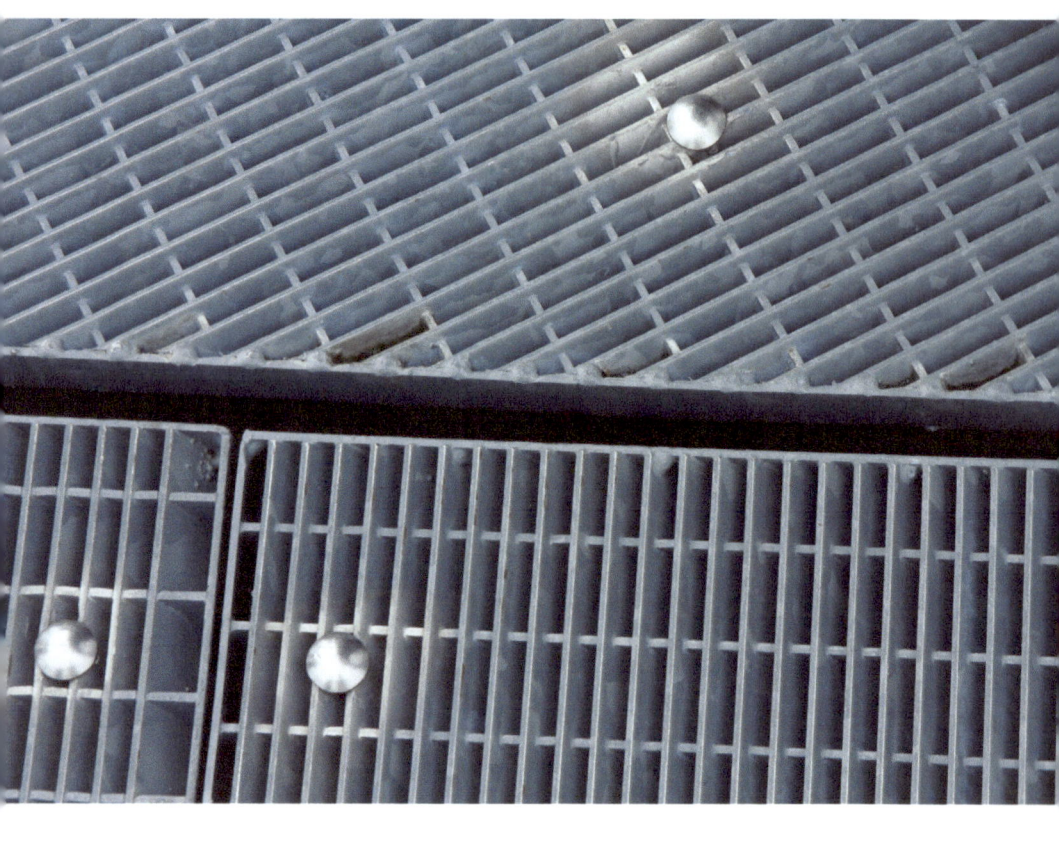

By the time he got home, Aesop was in tears and shaking.

He knew exactly what the story meant, even if his classmates hadn't figured it out yet.

Aesop had tried for days, but he found he couldn't force a story to serve his own ends without losing something of value. He could have come up with a dozen stories to keep him from being bullied, but none of them felt honest. And the stories he *did* come up with that felt true wouldn't help get the bullies off his case. Truth can't be special ordered, he thought bleakly.

If Aesop wanted the truth to be intact, he couldn't bend it to make it fit his own needs.

Aesop was miserable as he thought about Tad down at the swamp, hoping to find frogs to get him luck. Aesop had no idea if that would work or not. But Aesop vowed that from now on he wouldn't tell a story unless he was sure it was true.

Tomorrow, he thought, he was going to be beat up bad.

At lunchtime the next day, Javan again pushed Aesop into the center of the students. Aesop was no longer staring at the ground. He was pretty sure he was going to have the whole school against him in a minute or two. Better to get it over with.

"I have a riddle," Aesop said. "Why did the jackal eat his lunch?"

All his classmates said, in unison, "Because of what the rooster said."

Aesop grinned. At least this part he could enjoy.

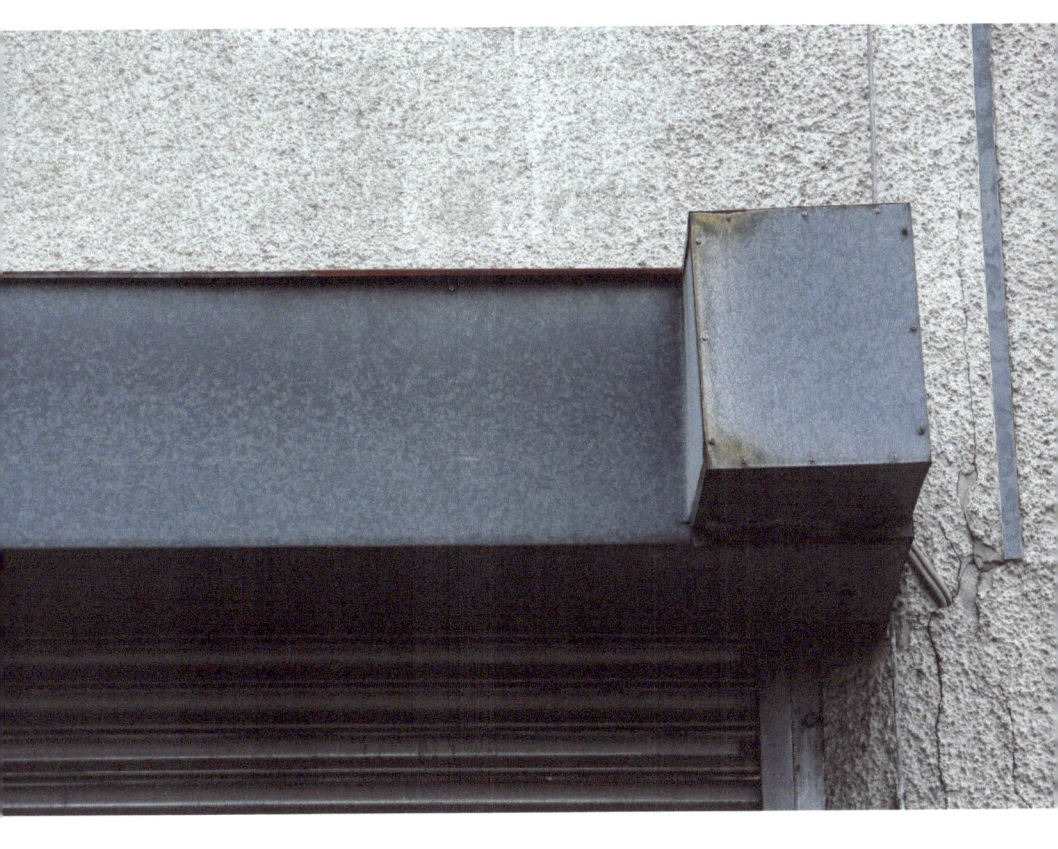

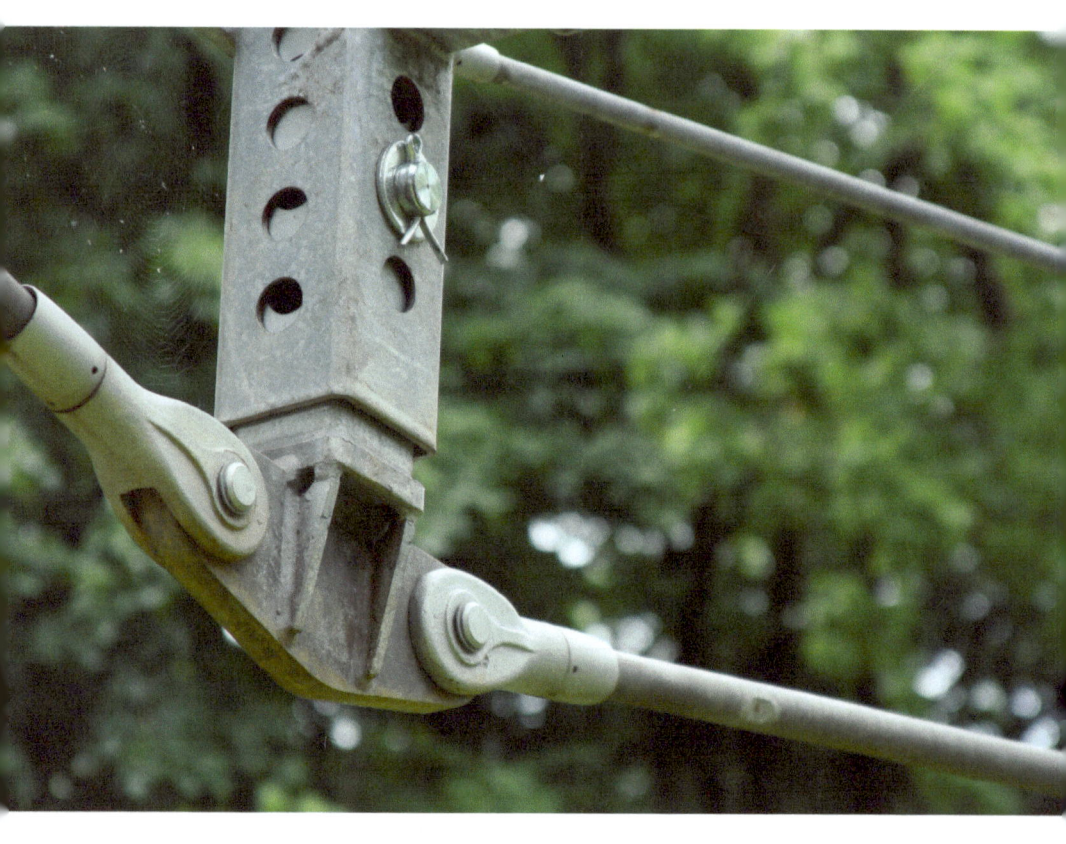

"You probably don't know what the rooster said," Aesop said.

"Truth can't be special ordered," everyone yelled.

"Maybe," Aesop said, "Maybe you don't know what that means. Any guesses?"

He asked this, hoping someone's response might bail him out.

"It means you're going to get beat up if you don't tell us," said Damian. A couple students snickered.

"I might get beat up even if I *do* tell you," Aesop responded, and a few more of the students laughed. Aesop wasn't the only one who had been bullied.

But Gina had an answer for Aesop's question. Gina had not liked what had been served for lunch that day and had asked for something different. She was told she could eat what was there or go hungry.

"I think," Gina said, "I think it means that truth is like the school lunch. You may not like it, but it's all you get. You have to take it or leave it," she said.

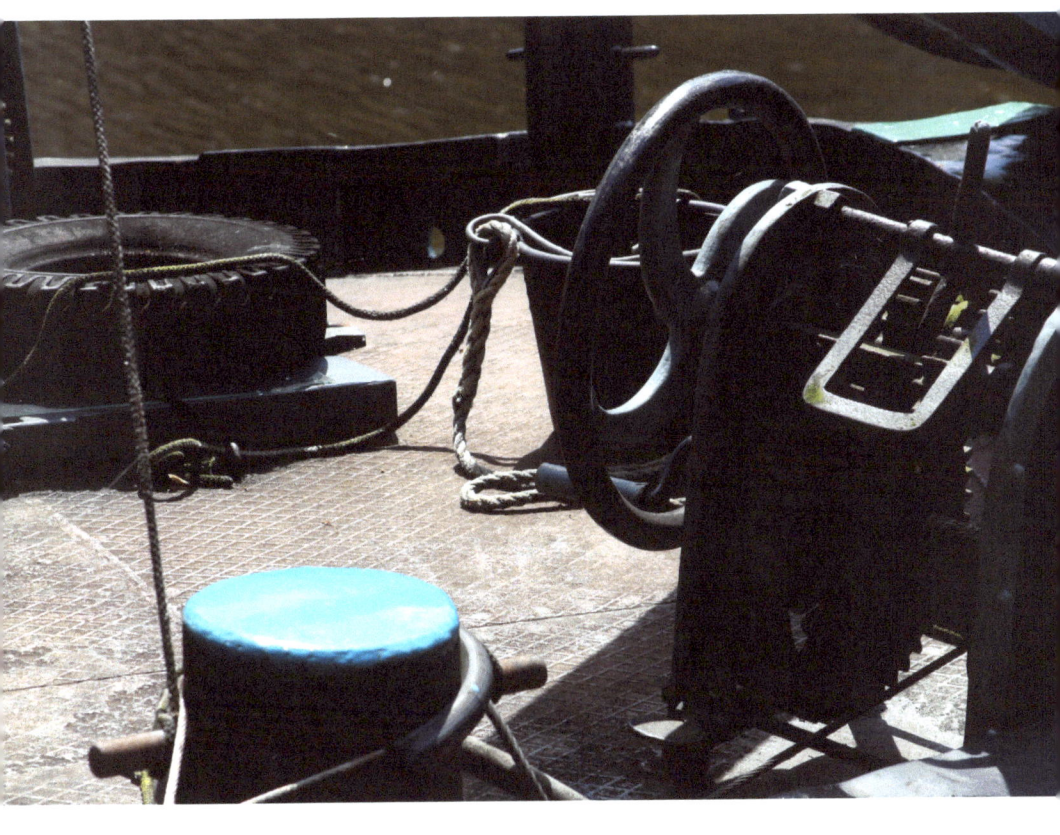

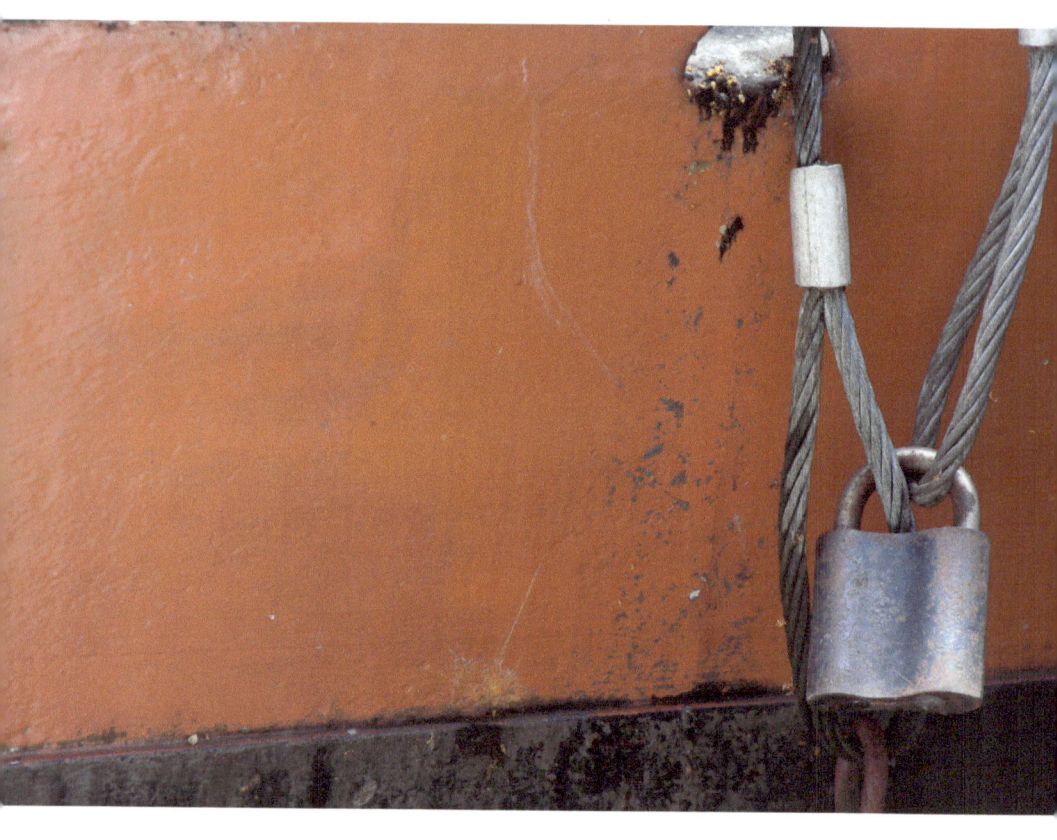

Aesop breathed a sigh of relief. That, he thought, was a way the riddle could be understood by all.

"That's right," said Aesop. "If you try to change the truth, what you have may be interesting. It may even be believable. But it's not the truth. If you want truth, you have to take it as it is. You can't change it to suit you and still have truth. You can't special order it."

That afternoon, Aesop walked all the way home without seeing Javan or Damian. They were down at the swamp, looking for Tad.

Aesop hadn't been beat up several days in a row. Things were looking up, he thought.

~~

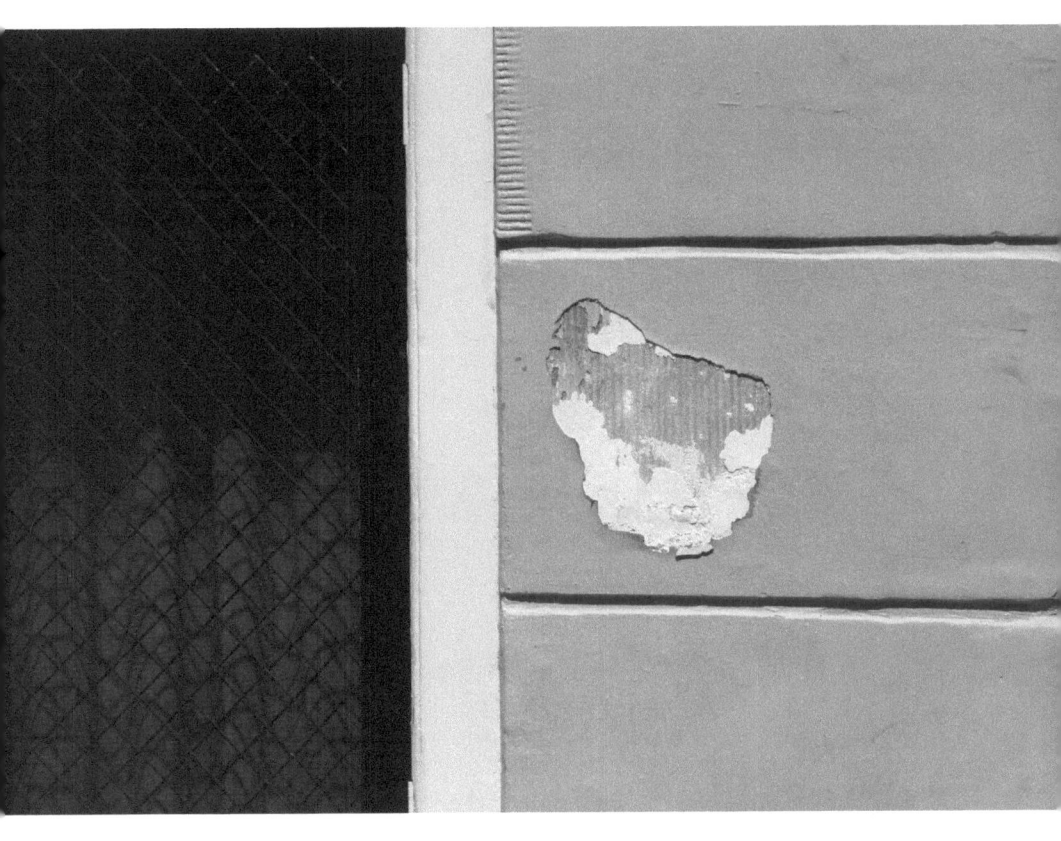

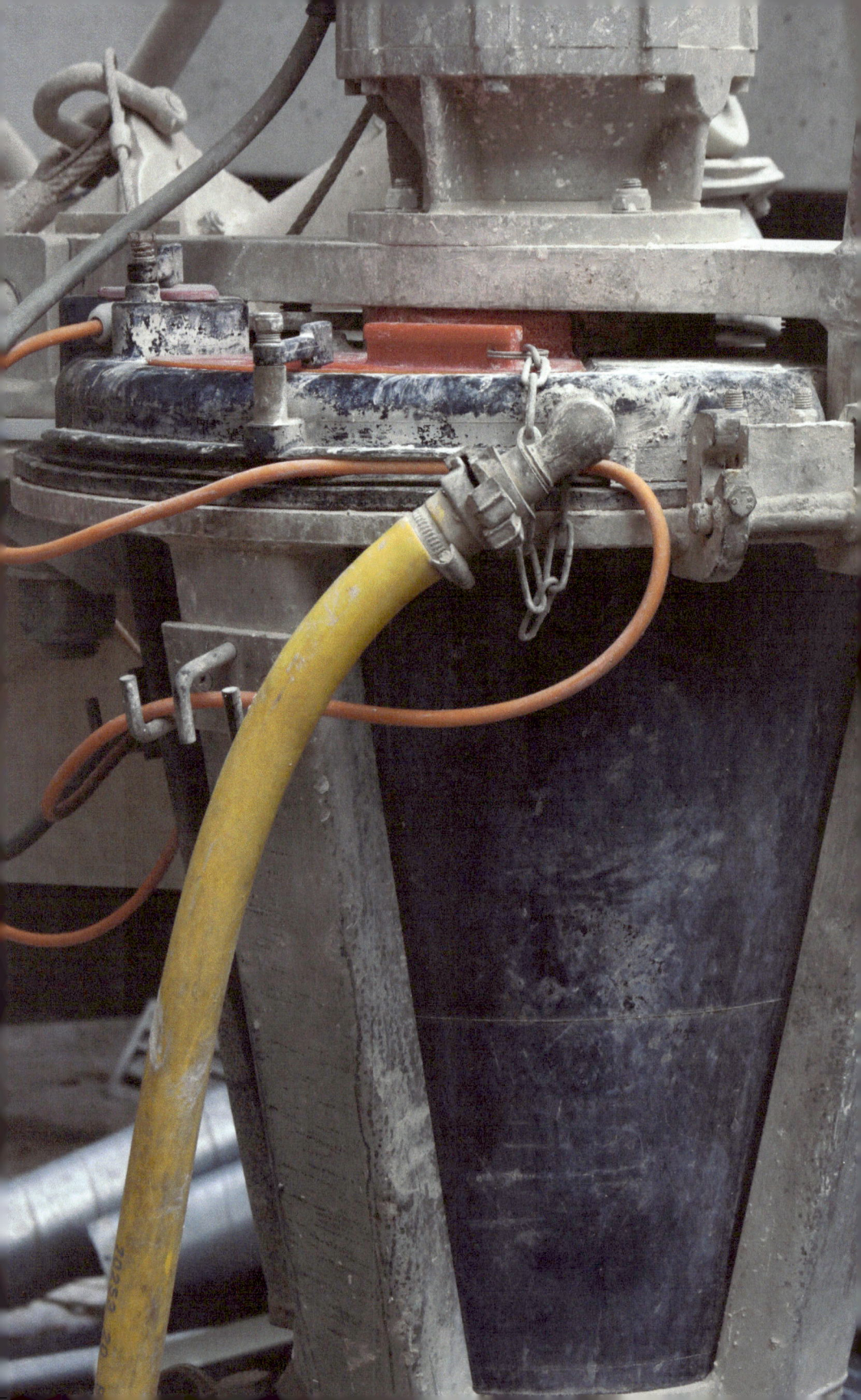

Reflection questions

Aesop tried to find something to say that would keep him from trouble. He had a long time to prepare. But when the time came, he still had nothing. So he blurted out the first thing that came into his head.

What do *you* do when you think you have nothing? Do you give up? Keep trying anyway?

For a while Aesop didn't see any change in his relationship with Javan and Damian. Sometimes change happens slower than we'd like. What changes would you like to see in your world?

What could you do to help start those changes?

What do you think of Aesop's belief that you can't change truth to suit yourself and still have truth?

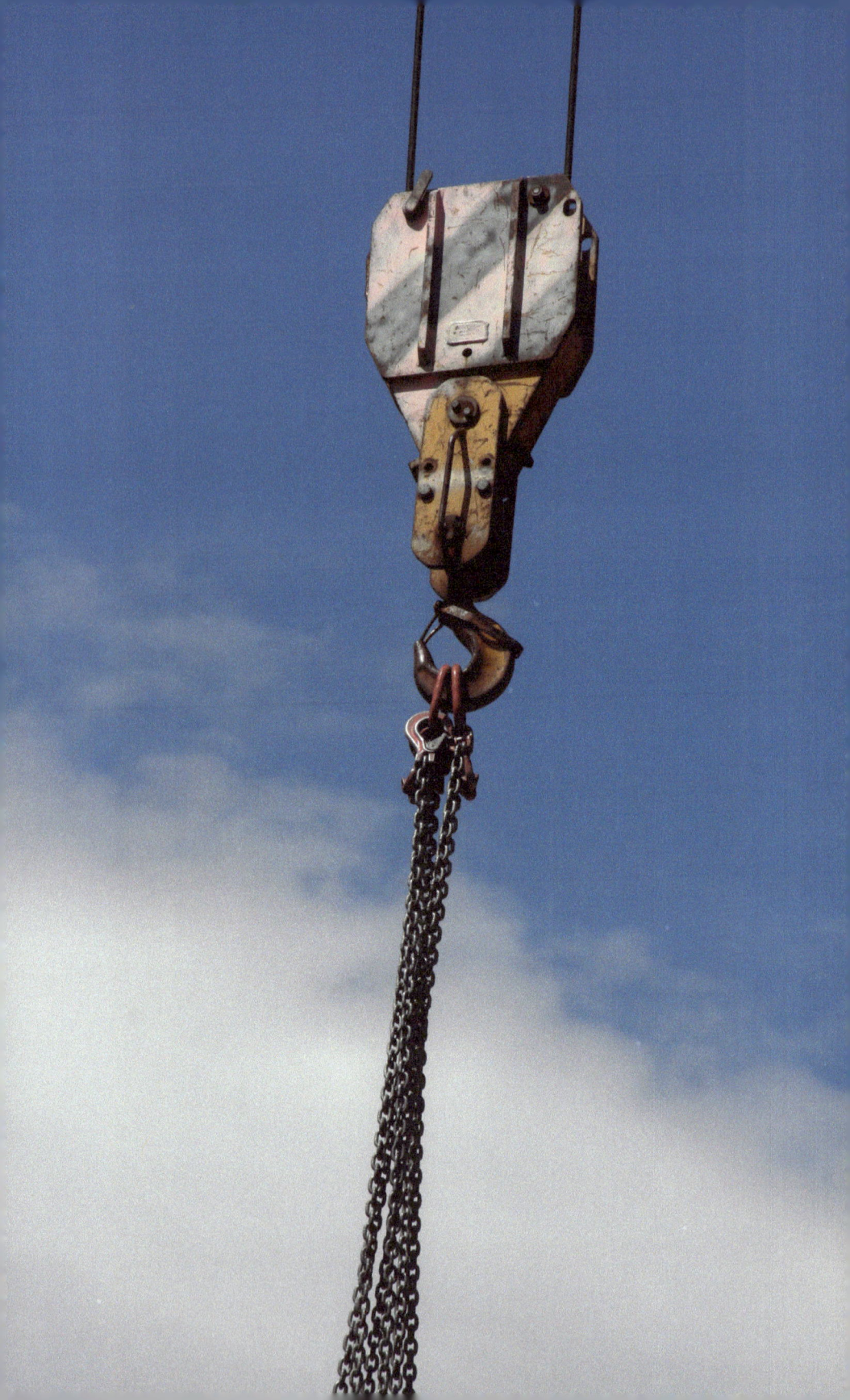

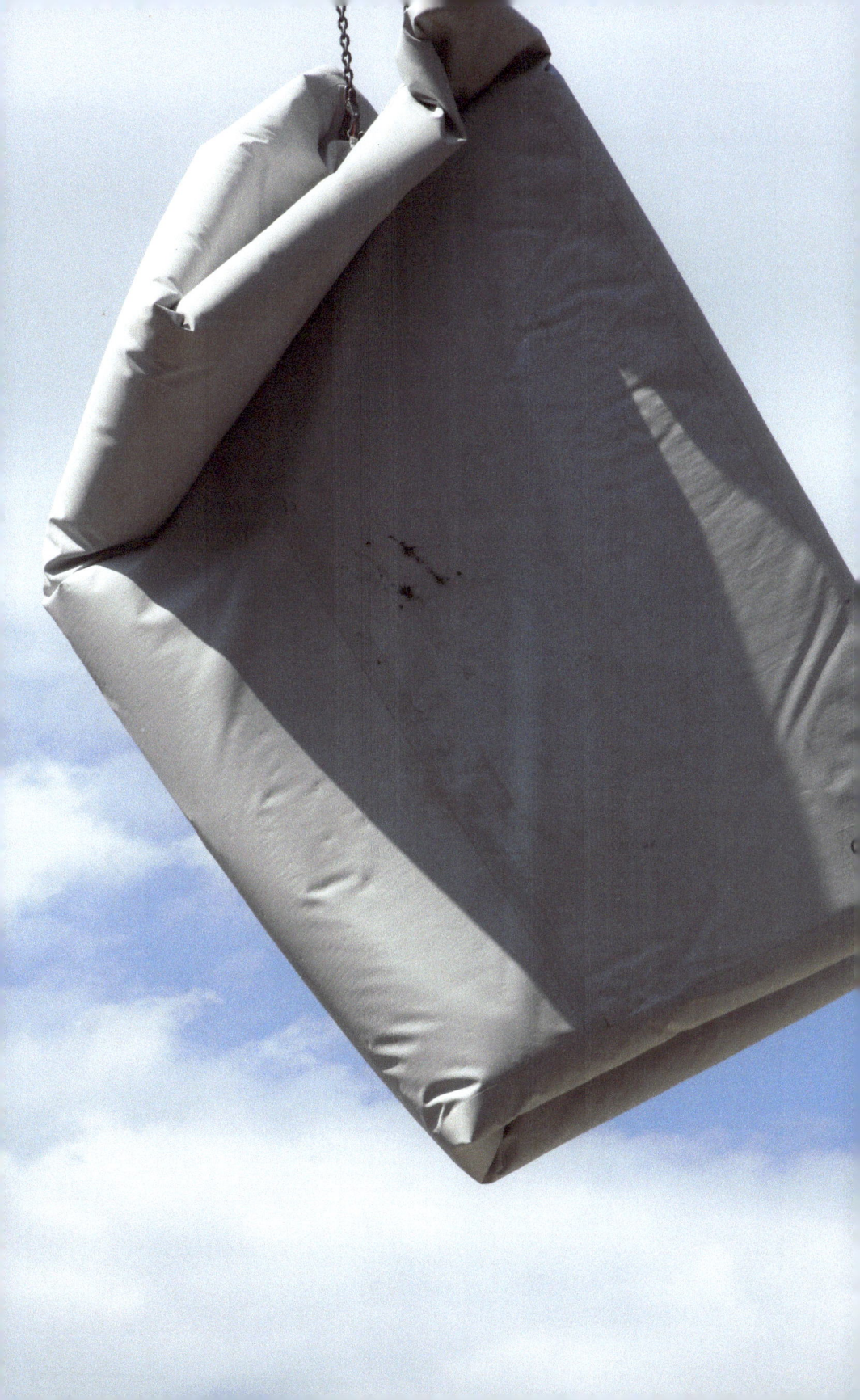

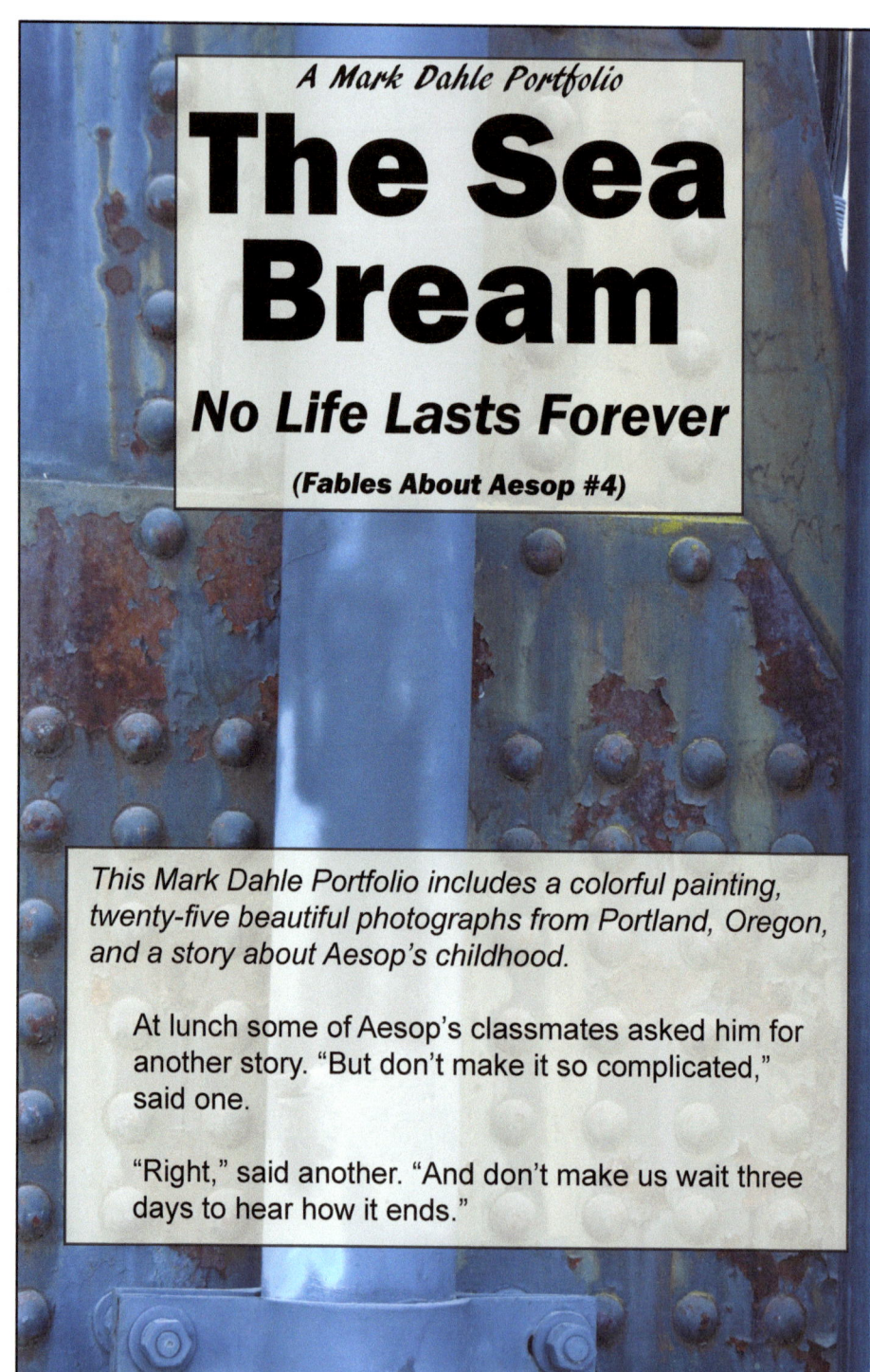

A Mark Dahle Portfolio

The Sea Bream

No Life Lasts Forever

(Fables About Aesop #4)

This Mark Dahle Portfolio includes a colorful painting, twenty-five beautiful photographs from Portland, Oregon, and a story about Aesop's childhood.

At lunch some of Aesop's classmates asked him for another story. "But don't make it so complicated," said one.

"Right," said another. "And don't make us wait three days to hear how it ends."

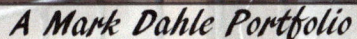

Tad And The Frogs

Friends Can Be Found In Unusual Places

(Fables About Aesop #5)

This Mark Dahle Portfolio includes a colorful painting, twenty-five beautiful photographs from Freiburg, Germany and Hawaii, and a story about Aesop making some unusual friends.

Octavia held Tad's shirt. Tad had written "I'm with Aesop" in big letters on the front.

"What does *that* mean?" she asked.

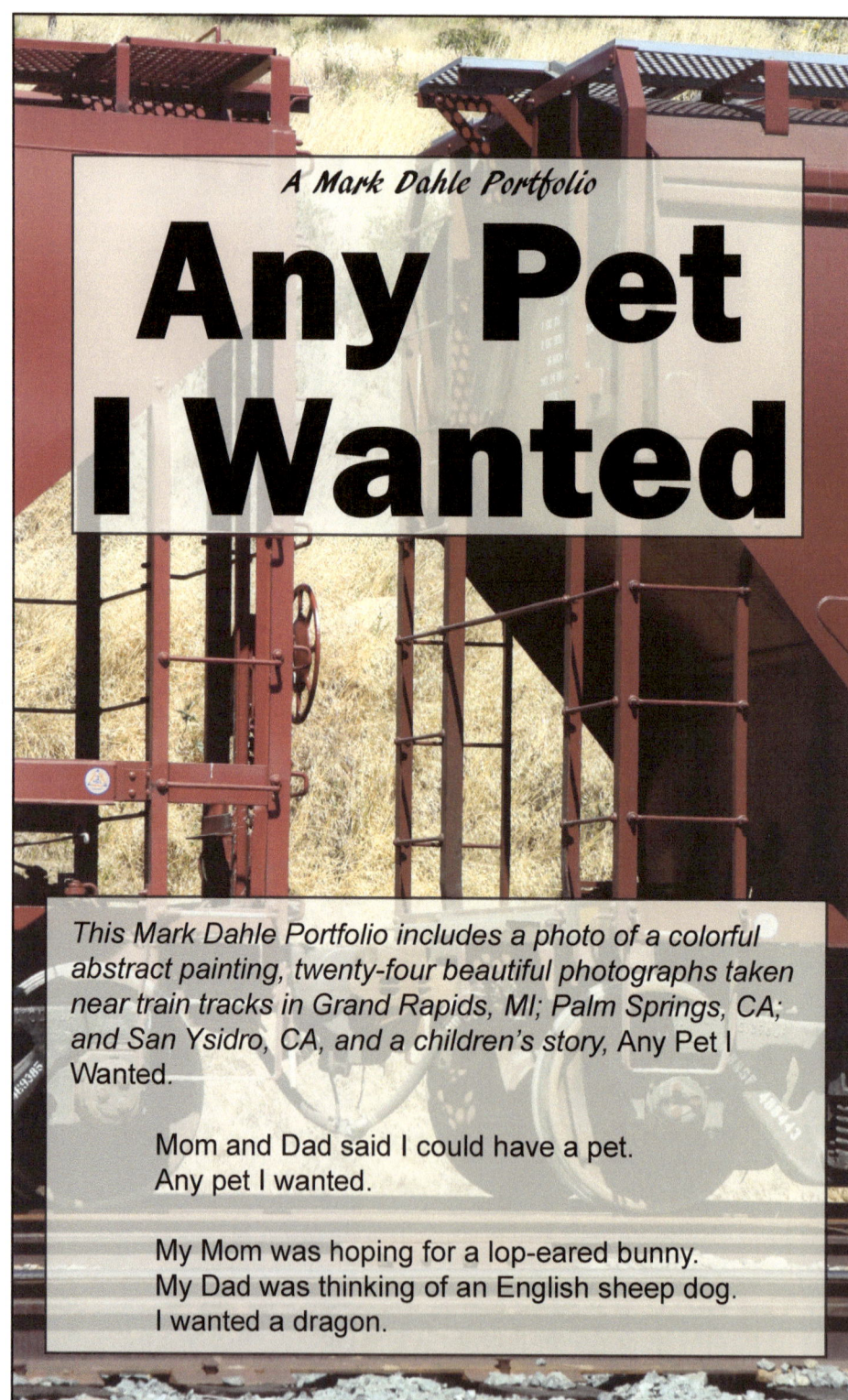

A Mark Dahle Portfolio

Any Pet I Wanted

This Mark Dahle Portfolio includes a photo of a colorful abstract painting, twenty-four beautiful photographs taken near train tracks in Grand Rapids, MI; Palm Springs, CA; and San Ysidro, CA, and a children's story, Any Pet I Wanted.

> Mom and Dad said I could have a pet.
> Any pet I wanted.
>
> My Mom was hoping for a lop-eared bunny.
> My Dad was thinking of an English sheep dog.
> I wanted a dragon.

www.ingramcontent.com/pod-product-compliance
Lightning Source LLC
Chambersburg PA
CBHW040902180526
45159CB00001B/497